One W🌐rld

THE HISTORY AND GOVERNMENT OF
Southwest Asia
and North Africa

AMANDA VINK

PowerKiDS
press™

Published in 2021 by The Rosen Publishing Group, Inc.
29 East 21st Street, New York, NY 10010

First Edition

Editor: Caitie McAneney
Book Design: Seth Hughes

Photo Credits: Cover (top) Mo Azizi/Shutterstock.com; cover (bottom) givaga/Shutterstock.com; p. 5 pingebat/Shutterstock.com; p. 6 David Steele/Shutterstock.com; p. 7 Dorling Kindersley/Getty Images; pp. 8, 16 Print Collector/Hulton Archive/Getty Images; pp. 10, 15 Universal History Archive/Universal Images Group/Getty Images; p. 11 Roger Wood/Corbis Historical/Getty Images; p. 12 (top) Waj/Shutterstock.com; p. 12 (middle) bumihills/Shutterstock.com; p. 12 (bottom) Fine Art/Corbis Historical/Getty Images; p. 14 (top left) ullstein bild/Getty Images; p. 14 (top right) ullstein bild/DEA/ARCHIVIO J. LANGE/De Agostini/Getty Images; p. 14 (bottom) Jean-Philippe Tournut/Moment/Getty Images; p. 17 lighthunteralp/Shutterstock.com; p. 19 SJ Travel Photo and Video/Shutterstock.com; p. 21 ullstein bild Dtl./Getty Images; p. 22 FRANCOIS GUILLOT/AFP/Getty Images; p. 23 Nicku/Shutterstock.com; p. 24 Izzet Keribar/Stone/Getty Images; p. 26 (top) Everett Historical/Shutterstock.com; p. 26 (bottom) https://upload.wikimedia.org/wikipedia/commons/1/17/Califate_750.jpg; p. 28 (top) DEA/G. DAGLI ORTI/De Agostini/Getty Images; p. 28 (bottom) Hulton Archive/Getty Images; p. 29 Historical Picture Archive/Corbis Historical/Getty Images; p. 30 Sepia Times/Universal Images Group/Getty Images; p. 32 Heritage Images/Hulton Fine Art Collection/Getty Images; p. 33 Peter Hermes Furian/Shutterstock.com; p. 35 Keystone-France/Gamma-Keystone/Getty Images; p. 36 (top) Oscar Marcus/Hulton Royals Collection/Getty Images; p. 36 (bottom) https://upload.wikimedia.org/wikipedia/commons/1/10/Middle_east_1914.jpg; p 38 GPO/Hulton Archive/Getty Images; p. 39 (top) Topical Press Agency/Hulton Archive/Getty Images; p. 39 (bottom) Bettmann/Getty Images; p. 40 Henryk Sadura/Moment/Getty Images; p. 42 https://upload.wikimedia.org/wikipedia/commons/7/70/Tunisie_President_Ben_Ali.jpg; p 44 (top) YASIN AKGUL/AFP/Getty Images; p. 44 (bottom) Tolga Sezgin/Shutterstock.com; p. 45 (top) Pajor Pawel/Shutterstock.com; p. 45 (bottom) shutterlk/Shutterstock.com.

Cataloging-in-Publication Data
Names: Vink, Amanda.
Title: The history and government of Southwest Asia and North Africa / Amanda Vink.
Description: New York : PowerKids Press, 2021. | Series: One world | Includes glossary and index.
Identifiers: ISBN 9781725321328 (pbk.) | ISBN 9781725321342 (library bound) | ISBN 9781725321335 (6 pack) | ISBN 9781725321359 (ebook)
Subjects: LCSH: Middle East–Juvenile literature. | Middle East–History–Juvenile literature. | Middle East–Politics and government–Juvenile literature. | Africa, North–Juvenile literature. | Africa, North–History–Juvenile literature. | Africa, North–Politics and government.
Classification: LCC DS62.V56 2021 | DDC 956–dc23

Manufactured in the United States of America

CPSIA Compliance Information: Batch #CSPK20: For Further Information contact Rosen Publishing, New York, New York at 1-800-237-9932

Find us on

CONTENTS

Introduction...**4**
Southwest Asia and North Africa

Chapter One... **7**
The Cradle of Civilization

Chapter Two..**13**
The Clash of Empires

Chapter Three.. **20**
The Rise of Islam

Chapter Four.. **27**
The Ottoman Empire

Chapter Five...**34**
Into the 20th Century

Chapter Six **40**
A Changing Region

Glossary... **46**

For More Information................................. **47**

Index...**48**

Introduction

SOUTHWEST ASIA AND NORTH AFRICA

Southwest Asia and North Africa is a region with a rich history dating back many thousands of years. As the first site of complex urban centers, this area today is home to varied and rich landscapes, cultures, traditions, resources, and religions. This diversity has shaped the political structures, policies, and aspects of everyday life there. Many nations in southwest Asia and North Africa are heavily governed by ancient traditions, with the religion Islam being of utmost importance.

Nearly six percent of the entire world's population lives within the region's many countries. Historically, southwest Asia and North

diversity: Exhibiting a variety of types.

Southwest Asia and North Africa include the countries of Bahrain, Cyprus, Egypt, Iran, Iraq, Israel, Jordan, Kuwait, Lebanon, Oman, Palestine, Qatar, Saudi Arabia, Syria, Turkey, United Arab Emirates (U.A.E.), and Yemen.

Africa have sat at the crossroads of the world's civilizations. Ancient trade routes, such as the Silk Road, connected this region to the rest of the world. The land has a variety of different geographical features, including deserts, mountains, and peninsulas. The region also holds valuable resources, like oil, which greatly affects the economy and government policies.

Southwest Asia and North Africa are commonly referred to collectively as the Middle East, a concept created by western occupation in the 19th and 20th centuries. This term is considered problematic by some, as it reflects European **colonialism** of the region.

The area has historically seen great conflict and rich cultures, which have shaped relationships in the local countries and the greater world.

Geographical features, like this desert in Saudi Arabia, have shaped life in the region for thousands of years, influencing trade, migration, borders, conflict, and the spread of ideas.

migration: Movement from one region to another.

Chapter One

THE CRADLE OF CIVILIZATION

The Fertile Crescent is a quarter-moon-shaped area reaching from the Persian Gulf to modern-day southern Iraq, Syria, Lebanon, Jordan, Israel, and northern Egypt. Since ancient times, life-bringing rivers created fertile, or rich, soils. The soil allowed farming communities to develop. Some of the oldest civilizations in the world grew out of these river valleys. These farming communities eventually led to the rise of urban centers. Scholars call this the Agricultural Revolution.

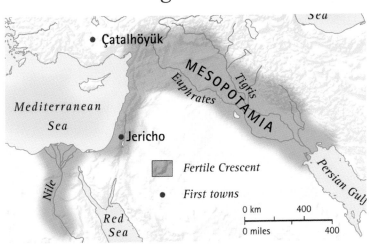

Early civilizations relied on their geographical landscapes to survive. For that reason, many ancient civilizations grew out of fertile river valleys, such as those in the Fertile Crescent.

Rising out of the Fertile Crescent, Mesopotamia was the site of many world firsts: the first use of math, laws, and the wheel. Ancient people perfected farming methods; they **domesticated** sheep and pigs, and developed systems of irrigation.

This artifact from an ancient royal tomb in Ur—today's southern Iraq—depicts domesticated animals and other goods being carried for a celebratory feast.

The Sumer civilization, the earliest known peoples in Mesopotamia, arose around 5,000 BC. One of the larger city-states, called Uruk, may have had as many as 80,000 residents. Usually these cities had a walled center with a ziggurat in the middle. Although

irrigation: The watering of a dry area by man-made means in order to grow plants.

ziggurat: An ancient Mesopotamian temple consisting of a pyramid-shaped structure built in stages with a shrine at the top.

the Sumerians shared a common language—and an early writing form called cuneiform—the city-states were often at war with one another. While Sumerians may have invented military tactics, like the **phalanx formation**, the divisions between the city-states made them **vulnerable** to attacks from outside forces.

History in F☉CUS

Ancient Mesopotamia and Egypt were **polytheistic**. Religion was an important part of everyday life. It was important to please the gods, who would grant good weather and crops.

Babylon, a Mesopotamian city near the Euphrates River, survived from the 18th to 6th centuries BC, and, at one point, held a population of an estimated 200,000 people. It was founded by the Akkadian Empire in northern Mesopotamia, and became a major military power under the rule of Hammurabi from 1792 to 1750 BC. Hammurabi conquered neighboring city-states, and the Babylonian Empire formed. This is the site of one of the first written legal codes, or laws, known as Hammurabi's Code.

History in F⬤CUS

The Code of Hammurabi was one of the first sets of written legal codes. One of the most famous of the 282 codes translates to "an eye for an eye," which demonstrates the law of **retribution**.

The stele, or pillar, containing the Code of Hammurabi depicts the ruler addressing a god directly, showcasing his unlimited power and authority.

EGYPTIAN DYNASTIES

Ancient Egypt was ruled over by a pharaoh, whom the people believed was a living god. Ancient Egypt was a theocracy and an unlimited government—the pharaoh's word was unquestioned. The first pharaohs established dynasties, or systems of rule that passed down generation to generation. Over the course of Egypt's history, 31 different dynasties ruled over the land.

Pharaohs planned complex burial chambers with great care. Early on, they built mastabas, or flat-roofed buildings. Later, pharaohs had grand pyramids built in their honor, filled with riches for the afterlife. In addition, they ordered architecture of all kinds to be created, from large statues to **obelisks** to huge buildings.

theocracy: Government of a state by divine guidance.

unlimited government: In an unlimited government, control is placed solely with the ruler and their appointees, and there are no limits imposed on their authority.

Ramses II, or Ramses the Great, took 20 years to build his temple at Abu Simbel in Egypt. The impressive temple is located on the Nile River.

In North Africa starting around 5500 BC, two major kingdoms developed along the Nile–Upper Egypt and Lower Egypt. Around 3200 BC, these two kingdoms came together under one ruler, King Narmer. This is recognized as the beginning of the Egyptian civilization. The Nile was extremely important to Egypt. Each year the waters flooded at a **predictable** rate and created ideal growing conditions. The Nile also became important for transporting goods and people, making the Egyptians very powerful.

The Pyramids of Giza are some of the most famous architectural structures in the world. They were built by three pharaohs between around 2550 and 2490 BC.

This step pyramid is composed of six mastabas.

The Rosetta Stone is currently on display at the British Museum in London, England.

THE ROSETTA STONE

The artifacts and buildings of the ancient Egyptians have stood the test of time. Their building materials were largely stone, and the dry desert climate preserved many artifacts.

In 1799, soldiers led by the French ruler Napoléon Bonaparte found the Rosetta Stone in Egypt. The Rosetta Stone is a large stone slab with three different languages on it: **hieroglyphics**, demotic (ancient Egyptian), and ancient Greek. When the stone was discovered, the knowledge of reading ancient Egyptian hieroglyphs had been lost. However, since scholars could understand ancient Greek, they were able to decode the ancient hieroglyphs.

Chapter Two

THE CLASH OF EMPIRES

Some people refer to the Persian Empire as the world's first superpower. It began as a collection of seminomadic tribes. The ancient Achaemenid tribe in present-day Iran defeated nearby kingdoms, including Babylon. In 550 BC, king Cyrus the Great created the first Persian Empire by joining the kingdoms under the rule of one dynasty. Also known as the Achaemenid Empire, the Persian Empire expanded, and civilizations within the region—Mesopotamia, Egypt, and India—were united.

seminomadic: Having to do with people who move from place to place seasonally, but who have a base camp where they cultivate some crops.

The ancient Persian capital city of Persepolis was named a UNESCO World Heritage Site in 1979. Ancient stone carvings can still be found there.

Darius the Great ruled from 522 BC to 486 BC, during the height of the Persian Empire. He introduced a standard currency and a measurement system. Trade flourished over roads that stretched across the empire. Persian artists created elaborate rock carvings, weaving, architecture, and metalwork.

History in F◉CUS

The Behistun Inscription was incredibly important for modern historians in understanding cuneiform, or wedge-shaped marks on clay tablets. It was carved into Mount Behistun in today's western Iran, and it told of Darius the Great's virtues.

The Behistun Inscription is carved into Mount Behistun, which is located in the Kermanshah Province of modern-day western Iran.

Daily life was heavily defined by religion. The official religion was Zoroastrianism, one of the world's oldest monotheistic faiths. Zoroastrianism is dualistic, meaning that followers of the faith believe in good and evil. Zoroastrianism is still practiced today in parts of Iran and India. It's widely believed the Achaemenian kings were **tolerant** of other religions.

The nearby Roman Republic prospered around the same time as the Persian Empire, leading to a clash between the civilizations. In 480 BC, the first Persian Empire began to decline, after a failed military strike of Greece by Xerxes I. In 331 BC, the Greek king Alexander the Great defeated King Darius III's troops and claimed the Persian throne.

The "Alexander Mosaic" from around 310 BC shows Alexander the Great on horseback as he defeated Darius III.

monotheistic: Having to do with belief in one god.

THE ROMAN-PERSIAN WARS (92 BC – 627 AD)

War between the Romans and the Persians stretched for more than seven centuries—among the longest conflicts in history. Many cities, such as Constantinople (today's Istanbul, Turkey), traded hands multiple times. Neither side could hang on to their winnings for long. The conflict lasted from the early Roman Empire through the Byzantine Empire. The wars encompassed both dynasties of the Persian Empire—the Parthians and the Sassanids.

In the beginning, battles were mostly about territory and resources. Later, however, there were religious aspects involved in the conflicts of the region, as Muslim armies invaded in the 7th century.

(v) ROME v. PERSIA (SASSANIAN) circa 300 A.D.

This 1915 map shows the territories of two great rivals—the Roman and Persian Empires—around AD 300. The borders between the empires changed often as wars raged for more than 700 years.

The Roman Empire continued to expand until it was too large to be governed from one place. The western half of the empire continued to have its headquarters in Rome, while the eastern half was governed out of Byzantium (today's Istanbul, Turkey). In AD 476, the western half of the Roman Empire fell.

Hagia Sophia, a spectacular domed church in Istanbul, was built under the rule of Justinian I, which lasted from AD 527 to 565.

The eastern part of the empire, also called the Byzantine Empire, prospered for another 1,000 years. Christianity was the main religion of the empire, and under Justinian I, many great monuments, churches, and monasteries were built. However, Justinian I's spending led to large debts and an understaffed army. Attacks from the Persians and from Slavs were a constant threat. However, the larger threat to the Byzantine Empire was a new religion: Islam.

JUDAISM AND CHRISTIANITY

Judaism is one of the world's oldest monotheistic religions, dating back nearly 4,000 years. The main religious text of Judaism is the Torah. According to the Torah, God first revealed himself to Abraham, who became the founder of Judaism.

In the first century AD, a Jewish prophet named Jesus Christ was executed, or killed, by Romans in today's Israel. Christians, followers of Christianity, believe that Christ was the Son of God, sent to Earth to save the world. Many Jewish people believe Christ was a prophet, but not the Son of God. Christianity spread throughout the Roman Empire, and is now the most practiced religion in the world with more than 2 billion followers.

In the Israeli city of Jerusalem, all three major monotheistic religions have sacred sites: the Islamic Temple Mount, the Jewish Western Wall, and the Christian Church of the Holy Sepulchre.

History in F◉CUS

Jews living outside of their homeland (today's Israel) are called the Diaspora. Throughout history, Jewish people have been persecuted for their beliefs, which has forced migration to other lands. The Zionist movement aims to return Jewish people to their homeland.

persecute: To treat someone cruelly or unfairly, especially because of race or religious or political beliefs.

Chapter Three

THE RISE OF ISLAM

According to Islamic texts, the angel Gabriel visited the prophet Muhammad in Mecca (a city in today's Saudi Arabia) in AD 610. Gabriel ordered Muhammad to recite the words of Allah, or God. Muhammad became the founder of Islam, and gathered a following of believers, called Muslims. Between 624 and 628, Muslims were involved in battles for their survival against tribal leaders in Mecca who saw this religion as a threat to their way of life. In 630, Muslim armies marched into Mecca and conquered the city. Muhammad pardoned, or excused, many of the defeated leaders, and most of the Meccan population **converted** to Islam.

prophet: A member of some religions who delivers messages that are believed to have come from the divine.

THE FIVE PILLARS OF FAITH

The basic religious duties of Muslims are called the Five Pillars. The first pillar is *shahada*, or the belief that there is no god except Allah, and Muhammad is Allah's messenger. The second pillar is *salat*, or participating in ritual prayer five times a day, facing the city of Mecca. The third pillar is *zakat*, or giving charity to the poor. The fourth pillar is *sawm*, or fasting from dawn to sunset during the month of Ramadan (the ninth month of the lunar calendar). The fifth pillar is *hajj*, or traveling to Mecca at least once in a lifetime. Muslims who are unable to make the journey to Mecca are excused from *hajj*.

Muhammad spent the last ten years of his life as a military strategist. He fought eight major battles, led raids, and planned dozens of military operations. He transformed the armies of Arabia and society as a whole by creating an *ummah*, a community of believers. Before

This 1307 painting shows the prophet Muhammad as he appoints a successor, Ibn Abu Talib. The question of Talib's right to be Muhammad's successor led to a schism in Islam, between Shi'i and Sunni branches.

Muhammad died in 632, he chose four rulers to continue the religion, but a debate remained over who should take over. This led to a schism and two major sects emerged: the Shiites and the Sunnis, who now make up nearly 90 percent of Muslims in the world.

This Qur'an (also spelled Koran) is a sacred religious text, which Muslims believe records the most perfect words of Allah, or God, as told to Muhammad.

History in F◉CUS

While Judaism, Christianity, and Islam have differences, the religions are similar in many ways. They are the three largest of the Abrahamic religions, which means they all consider Abraham as their first prophet.

schism: A formal division among members of a group that occurs because they disagree on something.

This 1885 illustration depicts the prophet Abraham. Worshippers of Judaism, Christianity, and Islam all believe Abraham was a prophet.

Islam expanded rapidly across southwest Asia and North Africa. Two years after Muhammad died, most of the Arabian Peninsula had converted. The Arab armies invaded Persian lands. In 642, the Muslim army won at Isfahan (in today's Iran), and in 643, they won at Herat (in today's Afghanistan).

History in F⦿CUS

Islam is the second-largest religion in the world, behind Christianity. It has about 1.8 million followers. There are many other sects, or divisions, inside the religion today, and each has its own set of customs and belief systems.

Nations governed by Islamic law, called caliphates, were established. They were under the leadership of caliphs. These began as **secular** positions, but over time they moved toward divine kingships, which claimed their only accountability was to God. These kinds of kingship demonstrate unlimited governments.

History in F⚙CUS

Many different languages are spoken in southwest Asia and North Africa today, but Arabic is most widely spoken, thanks to the spread of Islam throughout the region.

Built in 1228, the Divrigi Great Mosque and Hospital was a center for learning in today's Sivas, Turkey.

KNOWLEDGE IN THE ISLAMIC WORLD

Under the Abbasid Caliphate, from 750 to 1258, the world saw many advances in art, science, and commerce. The advances were inspired by verses from the Qur'an (the holy book of Islam) and Hadith (records of the words and actions of Muhammad) that spoke of the value of knowledge.

The Islamic world during this time was home to many different ethnic groups—Arabs, Persians, Egyptians, Turks, Armenians, and Jews. Using the knowledge of many cultures, the Islamic world developed in ways never before seen.

Physicians, mathematicians, and thinkers from Islamic countries were widely respected. They created madrassas, or great schools built alongside mosques. In the 8th century, Caliph Harun Al-Rashid founded the House of Wisdom in Baghdad, Iraq.

The Golden Age of Islam lasted between AD 800 and 1258. During this time period, the region saw advances in medicine, mathematics, science, technology, and the arts. Until the 18th century, scholars and medical students studied *Al-Qanun fi al-Ribb* or the "Canon of Medicine," written by Ibn Sina (known as Avicenna), one of the greatest thinkers of the Islamic Golden Age.

mosque: A building that is used for Muslim religious services.

Ibn Sina was born in AD 980 near Bukhara, present-day Iran. He made advances in medicine, astronomy, and philosophy, and is sometimes called the "father of modern medicine."

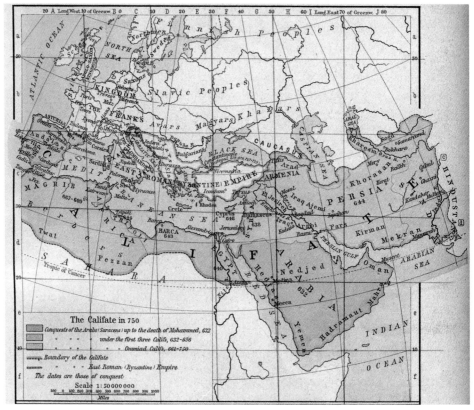

This map shows the extent of Islamic rule during the Golden Age of Islam, around the eighth century.

Chapter Four

THE OTTOMAN EMPIRE

In the 11th century AD, Seljuk Turkic tribes began to migrate into northwestern Persia. They defeated local rulers in Persia and prospered for two centuries.

History in F⊚CUS

The Seljuk (also spelled Seljuq) Turkic tribes were a nomadic people from Central Asia and southeast Russia. Their invasion of southwest Asia in the 11th century led to a rise in Turkish power in the region, laying the foundation for an empire that would span Mesopotamia, Palestine, Syria, and much of Iran.

THE CRUSADES AND JERUSALEM

Jerusalem has a long history of conflict, as the holy land for Muslims and Christians alike. In AD 1095, Pope Urban II called on Western Christians to take up arms to aid the Byzantines against Islamic forces and take back control of Jerusalem for Christians. There were eight violent military expeditions, called the Crusades, between 1095 and 1291.

In 1099, Christian Crusaders and Byzantine forces worked together to capture Jerusalem. The Battle of Hattin in 1187 allowed Islamic forces—led by Saladin, sultan of Egypt—to take back Jerusalem and other Holy Land cities. As part of the Third Crusade (1189–1192), Christian armies tried to recapture Jerusalem, but they did not succeed.

This painting depicts the surrender of Christian Crusade leader Richard the Lionheart to Muslim leader Saladin after the Battle of Hattin, which secured Jerusalem for the Muslims.

Pope Urban II ordered the First Crusade in AD 1095, which increased tensions between Christians and Muslims for hundreds of years.

In the 13th century, the Mongol invasion began. The Mongols were a group of nomadic tribes from Central Asia unified into one great army by Genghis Khan (1162–1227). The Mongols defeated the Seljuk Turks and gradually took over most of the Islamic world. It wasn't until 1260 that the Mongols were defeated by the Mamluks out of Egypt. The Mongol Empire began to decline in the 14th century. As multiple empires weakened and fell, the Ottoman Empire made its own advances in the region.

This engraving shows a janissary commander from the Ottoman Empire. Janissaries were members of the Turkish infantry, an elite fighting force used by the Ottoman Empire from the 14th to 19th centuries. They were the first modern army in Europe.

Developments in every artistic field took place during the Ottoman Empire. This photograph shows a Turkish carpet from around 1575.

The Ottoman Empire was created by Turkish tribes in Anatolia around AD 1299. Its founder was Osman I. He expanded the borders of his territory and took over the Byzantine district of Bithynia, an important position on the Black Sea. The Ottomans attracted rivals of the powerful Byzantine Empire—which, when defeated, expanded the Ottoman Empire significantly. In 1453, the Ottoman Empire captured the major Byzantine capital of Constantinople. This was the end of the Byzantine Empire.

ISLAM AND THE BYZANTINE EMPIRE

In AD 629, the prophet Muhammad sent a letter to Byzantine Emperor Heraclius, among others. The letter urged the Christian rulers to convert to Islam, but they refused.

Emperor Heraclius was one of the most powerful rulers in the world, and the Byzantine Empire controlled nearly all the land touching the Mediterranean. Sacred Christian artifacts were safe in Jerusalem under Byzantine control. Perhaps unsurprisingly, Heraclius did not convert.

By 644, Islamic armies had driven Byzantine forces from Egypt, Syria, and Mesopotamia. The Islamic armies built a new capital in Damascus (in today's Syria) and a new temple in Jerusalem.

Süleyman the Magnificent became sultan of the Ottoman Empire in 1520, leaving behind a powerful legacy. Early on, he ordered his armies to fight against Christian powers in

sultan: A king of a Muslim state.

legacy: Something that is passed down from someone.

central Europe, especially the Hapsburg Empire. The Ottoman Empire fought a series of wars that expanded their reach into Hungary and Greece. The naval strength of the Ottomans increased during Süleyman's rule, as they won a sea battle against the fleets of Venice and Spain in 1538. Istanbul (formerly Constantinople) became a center of trade and learning for the Turkish and Islamic Empire.

Under the rule of Süleyman the Magnificent from 1520 to 1566, the Ottoman Empire expanded its territories and established itself as a cultural center.

History in F◉CUS

At its height, the Ottoman Empire controlled the Arabian Peninsula, the area of the former Byzantine Empire, parts of Egypt, and even areas in southern Europe, including Hungary and the Balkans.

After the rule of Süleyman, the Ottoman Empire struggled to maintain its power as sultans lost loyalty and respect, and the empire lost key territories, such as Greece. The Tanzimat reforms of the mid-1800s were meant to modernize the empire through educational, political, and economic changes, but they only added to a debt crisis in the 1870s. It left the Ottoman Empire in a fragile state.

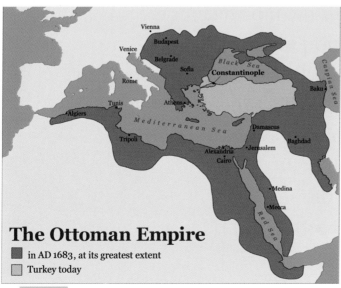

The Ottoman Empire

■ in AD 1683, at its greatest extent
□ Turkey today

The Ottoman Empire existed for over 600 years, acquiring lands across southwest Asia and North Africa.

reform: A change meant to improve things for the better.

Chapter Five

INTO THE 20TH CENTURY

The Tanzimat reforms from 1839 to 1876 tried to modernize the Ottoman Empire and protect it from colonial powers and nationalist movements. However, the Ottoman Empire struggled to maintain power in the late 19th century, as European forces colonized many areas between Morocco and Turkey. Conservative Islamic movements, like the Wahhabis movement on the Arabian peninsula, drew the line between those who would work with European powers and those who would oppose colonialism.

nationalist: Supporting national independence.

THE VALUE OF OIL

The natural resources of southwest Asia and North Africa are incredibly valuable, which encouraged colonization and international involvement over the years. Overuse and **scarcity** of these resources have created conflict that has shaped much of the modern Arabian Peninsula. Some countries within the region have huge revenues, or profits, from the sale of oil, while others, like Egypt, do not. Oil makes up more than 90 percent of the budget revenue for Saudi Arabia.

The Organization of Petroleum Exporting Countries (OPEC) was founded in 1960. Member countries include Iran, Iraq, Kuwait, and Saudi Arabia. The nations work together to determine oil prices and oversee oil production within the region.

History in F●CUS

Oil isn't the only valuable, scarce resource in the region—increasing desertification in the region has made freshwater harder to find, which sometimes leads to conflict. Desalinization plants operate in many countries, but they are not a permanent solution.

This photograph shows oil rigs in Saudi Arabia in the 1940s. The production of oil has shaped much of the region politically, and continues to do so today.

OPEC: A multinational group formed to coordinate worldwide petroleum policy and prices.

desertification: The process where fertile land turns into desert, usually caused by overgrazing.

desalinization: The process of removing salt from seawater to make freshwater.

Britain formally occupied Egypt and controlled its government from 1822 to 1922.

France colonized Tunisia in 1881, Britain colonized Egypt in 1882, and France and Spain overtook Morocco in 1912. In 1878, the Congress of Berlin declared the independence of Romania, Serbia, and Bulgaria. In 1912 and 1913, the Ottoman Empire lost nearly all territories in Europe during the Balkan Wars. However, it was World War I that marked the final end to the once-great empire.

In this 1914 map, British territories are in red and Ottoman territories are in purple. Soon after, the region was further broken up between European powers.

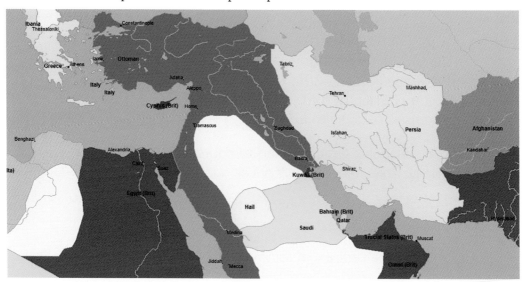

In 1914, World War I swept across the European continent. The Ottoman Turks entered the war on the side of the Central Powers, which included Germany and Austria-Hungary. The Central Powers were at war against the Allies, which included France, Italy, Russia, and the United States. When the Central Powers lost to the Allies in 1918, the Ottoman Empire was broken forever. In 1922, the title of "sultan" was officially removed, and the empire dissolved. Turkey was declared a republic in 1923.

Europeans colonized much of the Ottoman Empire during the 19th century. However, after World War I, there was a complete takeover of former Ottoman territories, with French and British armies and agents moving into southwest Asia and North Africa. In 1916, the French and British secretly negotiated the Sykes-Picot Agreement, which carved the Middle East (as it was now called) into spheres of influence. Russia acquired several Armenian provinces and Kurdish territories, France acquired Lebanon, and Great Britain acquired southern Mesopotamia.

History in F⊙CUS

Under the British Mandate for Palestine in 1939, the British government made Palestine a binational state for both Arabs and Jews, and they called for restrictions on Jewish immigration. This strained Jewish-Arab relations in the region. On May 14, 1948, the Jewish state of Israel declared its independence.

The Zionist movement gained strength during World War II and Hitler's attack against the Jewish people. Many Jewish people, like those in this photo, tried to return to their ancestral homeland.

The League of Nations was a world organization formed to resolve international disputes after World War I. The League adopted the mandate system, which said the Middle East should remain under the guidance of European powers until the countries were able to "stand alone." This was another form of colonialism, as European powers settled in for the long run.

immigration: The act of coming to a country to settle there.

The League of Nations was set up after World War I to maintain international peace. It was unsuccessful—World War II broke out two decades later.

THE PERSIAN GULF WAR

The remainder of the 20th century was defined by political divisions in the region. In 1980, Iraqi forces invaded western Iran, claiming that Iran had attacked border posts. The Iran-Iraq war lasted until 1988, resulting in more than a million casualties.

In 1990, Iraqi leader Saddam Hussein invaded Kuwait over disputes about oil prices, starting the Persian Gulf War. The United Nations Security Council demanded that Hussein's troops withdraw. In January 1991, the United States led a massive air strike called Operation Desert Storm. The attacks lasted 42 days, until Iraqi forces withdrew. The war would have lasting effects on the region.

Saddam Hussein rose to power beginning in 1976, as the general of Iraqi armed forces. He was executed in 2006 in Iraq for crimes against humanity.

Chapter Six

A CHANGING REGION

Southwest Asia and North Africa has a long history of diverse cultures, rich religious traditions, and ever-changing borders. Unrest in the region has changed government structures and functions. Because of this, there are many different kinds of governments and political structures in the region today.

MOROCCO

Tourists from all over the world come to southwest Asia and North Africa to experience the diverse cultures, grand architecture, and traditional foods.

Some countries are based on traditional principles and structures. Many of the countries within the region have governments that follow laws based on Islam, including Afghanistan, Iran, and Sudan. Saudi Arabia, Qatar, and Bahrain still have absolute monarchies, where rulers have authority to do whatever they want. Although they rule unchallenged, they sometimes follow the guidelines of religious leaders.

History in F⦿CUS

Over half the population of southwest Asia and North Africa lives in cities, with less than 10 percent living nomadic lifestyles. In 2018, Cairo had a population of over 9 million people.

Constitutional monarchies include Morocco, Jordan, Kuwait, and the United Arab Emirates. These limited governments have a written constitution to ensure that one person cannot hold too much power.

constitutional monarchy: A system of government in which a country is ruled by a king and queen whose power is limited by a constitution.

limited government: In a limited government led by the citizens, everyone, including all authority figures, must obey the laws.

President Zine al-Abidine Ben Ali became president of Tunisia in 1987 after peacefully overtaking the government.

Pro-democracy uprisings began in Tunisia in 2010, known as the Jasmine Revolution. People took to the streets to protest corruption in their government. Tunisian president Zine al-Abidine Ben Ali's rule bordered on dictatorship. Dozens of protesters were killed, attracting international attention. Because of this, Ben Ali stepped down, and an interim, or temporary, government was put in place. The interim government set up the country's first democratic parliamentary elections for a new government and a new constitution was drafted.

dictatorship: A government where the leader has unlimited power and severely limits the rights of the citizens.

MOHAMED BOUAZIZI AND THE JASMINE REVOLUTION

In 2010, 26-year-old Tunisian Mohamed Bouazizi was trying to make a living selling fruit from a cart. Local officials took what he was trying to sell, claiming he did not have the necessary permit to sell fruits and vegetables. Bouazizi took his case to the local government's office, but was denied a hearing. Later that same day, on December 17, 2010, Bouazizi set himself on fire outside the governor's office.

Many people in the country identified with Bouazizi. His death led to the Jasmine Revolution, and the wider movement in the region, called the Arab Spring, which fought against autocratic, or corrupt and unlimited, regimes.

History in F◉CUS

Today, Tunisia is a representative democratic republic and has three branches of government: executive, legislative, and judicial.

Pro-democracy uprisings followed in several countries—Egypt, Bahrain, Libya, Syria, and Yemen—in what would become known as the Arab Spring. Not all countries experienced lasting political change—and some are still experiencing violence. For example, authoritarian rule returned to Egypt after President Mubarak stepped down in 2011.

Since the fall of the Ottoman Empire, the region of southwest Asia and North Africa has changed politically many times—which often results in conflict zones, such as this town in Syria.

In Syria, a civil war that began in the aftermath of the Arab Spring continues. In northern Syria, a militant group called ISIS (Islamic State of Iraq and al-Sham) established a caliphate, or Islamic nation. ISIS committed many violent acts, and while weakened, continues to pose difficulties in the region. Under the rule of longtime dictator Bashar al Assad, who came to power in 2000, refugees from Syria have had to flee to other countries.

As history has demonstrated, from the Fertile Crescent to modern-day Syria, upheaval continues to drive political and social changes throughout southwest Asia and North Africa. Other countries, especially the United States, maintain strong military presences throughout the region, which strongly influence life and government

In this camp in Turkey, an estimated 28,000 Syrian refugees have found a temporary place to live.

structures there. As the region interacts with the wider world, more changes are sure to be on the horizon.

Citizens and tourists of southwest Asia and North Africa can enjoy diverse cultures and fun festivals, such as this fireworks display in Dubai.

History in F◉CUS

The COVID-19 global pandemic, which started in 2019, put stress on governments in this region and around the world that will continue to have lasting effects.

EVERYDAY MIDDLE EAST

Despite the upheaval that affects the region, it's important to remember that a rich culture remains. Not every moment of every day is filled with violence. The increased use of phones, internet, and apps allow many people to share the beauty and culture of the region today. To that end, a project called Everyday Middle East, which began in 2014, uses the hashtag #everydaymiddleeast to show individuals, music festivals, architecture, nature, schools, and nightlife. People can comment from all over the world, asking questions and clearing up **misconceptions** about the region's people and their homes.

An international business hub, Dubai is the largest and most populous city of the United Arab Emirates.

GLOSSARY

colonialism: Control by one country over another area and its people.

convert: To bring over from one belief, view, or party to another.

domesticate: To breed or train an animal for use by humans.

hieroglyphics: A writing style that uses characters that look like pictures.

misconception: A wrong or inaccurate idea.

obelisk: A column of stone with a square base, sides that slope in, and a pyramid on top.

phalanx formation: A body of troops or police officers standing or moving in close formation.

polytheistic: Believing in and worshipping multiple gods.

predictable: Happening in a way that's expected.

retribution: Punishment for doing something wrong.

scarcity: A condition where there is not enough of a product to meet demand for the product.

secular: Not religious.

tolerant: Willing to accept behaviors or feelings different from your own.

vulnerable: Open to attack or damage.

FOR MORE INFORMATION

BOOKS:

Clapper, Nikki Bruno. *Let's Look At Syria*. North Mankato, MN: Capstone Press, 2018.

Honovich, Nancy. *1,000 Facts About Ancient Egypt*. Washington, D.C.: National Geographic Children's Books, 2019.

Wilkinson, Philip. *Eyewitness Islam*. New York, NY: DK Publishing, 2018.

WEBSITES:

Food: Middle Eastern
www.pbs.org/food/cuisine/middle-eastern/
This webpage features recipes from the region of southwest Asia and North Africa.

Mesopotamia
www.dkfindout.com/us/history/mesopotamia/
Explore Mesopotamia's monuments, religion, and culture through images of how the early civilization may have looked.

What Is the Middle East?
teachmideast.org/articles/what-is-the-middle-east/
Read more about the area known as the Middle East.

INDEX

B

Babylon 9, 13
Byzantine Empire 16, 18,
    31, 33

C

Christianity 18, 22, 23
Crusades, the 28

E

Egypt 5, 7, 9, 10, 11, 12,
    13, 25, 28, 29, 31, 33,
    35, 36, 43

I

Islam 4, 18, 20, 21, 22, 23,
    24, 25, 26, 29, 31, 41
Islamic State of Iraq and al-
    Sham (ISIS) 44

J

Jasmine Revolution 42, 43
Judaism 18, 22, 23

L

League of Nations 38, 39

M

Mesopotamia 8, 9
Mongols 29
Muhammad 20, 21, 22,
    23, 31

O

Organization of Petroleum
    Exporting Countries
    (OPEC) 35
Ottoman Empire 27, 29,
    30, 31, 32, 33, 34, 36,
    37, 44

P

Palestine 5, 38
Persian Empire 13, 14, 15,
    16
Persian Gulf War 39

R

Rosetta Stone 12

W

World War I 36, 37, 38, 29
World War II 38, 39